Open Your Mind *Before* You Invest

Empowering the *Aspiring Investor*

By Roland Troutman

Open your mind before you invest
Empowering the Aspiring Investor

Written by: Roland Troutman
Art work by: Roland Troutman/ courtesy google free creation
logo artwork
Published by Trout House Publishing Company

ISBN 978-1-7341129-0-0

Always Put God First!

-Roland Troutman

This book is dedicated in the loving memory
of my grandmother, Nancy Pauline Sledge
my father, Roland E. Troutman Sr.
and my cousin Larry "Dee" Darden

Roland Troutman

Acknowledgments

First and foremost, I give all honor and praises to God for blessing me with the gifts of writing, arts, music, the art of selling and skills of business. Next, I want to give a super special thank you to my lovely wife, Jane, sweetheart for being in my corner throughout everything- I love you. Thank you to my grandfather, R.C. Sledge- for reading the Bible to me when I was a child, and you never gave up on me. Thank you to my mother, Bonnie Sledge for giving me life and hanging in there for as long as you could, I love you. Thank you, Linda Troutman, Tommie Troutman and Samuel Sledge for all of the love, support and lessons on life. Thank you to all of my partners and business associates. Thank you to the staff at Trout House Publishing's. Thank you, Susan Harring, for your hard work on all of my projects.

Shout outs to: Rolandia Troutman-Harris, Aundre Harris, Napoleon Sledge, Wil Darden, John and Sandra Parks, Tiffany Beeman, James Harrison, Shaneal Harrison, Michael Campbell and Stacy Diggs- Campbell, Bryan Rhuf, Alex Yount, Sheyna Yount, Amanda Yount, Rylei Troutman, Abel Mixaykham, Wade Hinds, Ted Beardsley, Chance the Rapper, Rappin' 4 Tay, Producer Talbot Snow- Las Vegas, Buck Wild, Marcus Adams- The Music Man, Pastor Marvin Williams, Pastor Jack, Pastor Darrell Delaney, Ced Glover, Producer Jay Collins- Ft. Meyers, Lori Troutman, Marcus Lemonis, Dwight Dunmire, Ryan Hollan, Xavier X-Man Goss, Leah Capetti, Jeez and Kee Jackson, Al Huppe, Alden Payne, Eniko Humphrey, Jason Peoples, Vernell Phipps, Roger Jackson, Shannon Cook, Govan McAbee, Blu, William Clay and Wayland Clay,

Jamal Troutman, Keith Troutman, Tyler Wilmer, Josh Hartman, Shawnette Davis, Sheldon and Sonya Surles, and all of the friends and family that I didn't mention, it's all love.

Contents

- 1 -
Key Factors for Any Business

Thank you for taking the time to invest in your future. You're probably wondering, "what in the world is Roland talking about?" Well if you are reading this book, then you must care enough about yourself that you want to expand your horizon, make more money, open up a business, and become a better over-all person. My first book, "Open Your Mind Before Your Business," was about building a foundation. It was about tapping into our inner-self, that God force that dwells deep within our souls and making our dreams become a reality. It was also a combination of spiritual motivation mixed with business information and strategy. Open your mind before your business was an introductory blueprint of effective processes for sales and business.

This book is intended to show you where the money is and the primary functions of the United States federal banking system. I'm going to show you how to keep the cashflow flowing, while expanding your empire. Along the way, we'll cover the science of investing, investment strategies and what to invest in. We are also going to discuss partnerships and deals gone bad.

A fluid cashflow is the most crucial part of any business

for long term sustainability. A fluid cashflow means that your company has the capability to keep the money flowing and working through various financial strategies and privileged investments. A fluid cashflow will also give you the means to handle unforeseen emergencies. Having credit will give you buying power and the ability to survive during slow times like a recession or stock market crash.

Fluids in a bottle are constantly moving around-creating motion-energy. The energy is the profits-a return on your investment. However, the lack of cash or credit can shut your business down within a month. I emphasize the importance of credit because without sufficient credit to sustain the bleeding, your business will suffer an agonizing demise. The bleeding that I'm referring to can come in many forms such as loss of cash, decline in sales, shrinkage, poor customer service, unfair prices, cheaper competition, advertising cost, unpaid taxes, collections from creditors, mis-use of funds, no insurance, no surety bond, bad partnership deals, and good ole fashioned lawsuits. Going into business isn't for everyone. Investing isn't for everyone. Without proper knowledge and guidance – you could very well end up with a handful of missed opportunities instead of a fistful of dollars.

<u>A few more reasons why cashflow and credit are essential</u> for any business:
- In order to meet supply and demand of goods/services.
- To cover employee payroll, government taxes, Insurances and operating expenses.
- For expansion and over-all financial growth.
- For company stability and future investment strategies.

I want to reiterate the importance of fluid cashflow and excellent credit because without it, your business may not be capable of meeting supply and demand for goods and services. You may accrue astronomical amounts of debt and acquire bad credit that may force your business into bankruptcy. Due to lack of sales and poor service you may be forced to go out of business as quick as you opened. Finally, there is a chance of potential lawsuits due to breach of contract with vendors, creditors and partners.

Over the years, I've seen many businesses crippled from the lack of adequate cashflow. And when businesses closed their doors and went out of business, no one gave a second thought about the employees whose lives were ravaged in the blink of an eye. We're going to discuss how to obtain the funds you need to make your business a reality. We'll also talk about payroll, operational requirements, taxes, insurances, permits, licenses, DBA's and much more. SO, LETS GET STARTED!

Before you can open a business, you must have an effective, bulletproof, business plan. This plan should give a breakdown as to how you will finance your company, as well as explain your product and processes. It is rare that any lender or investor will put up all of the required capital for any business to start, sustain or expand. The majority of the time investors are looking to invest in businesses that have already made significant sales and have been in business for two or more years. If you are a startup business, typically investors and lenders will want you to come up with 30 to 50 percent of the required funding as stated within your business plan. In exchange for the money, in some cases, the lender/investor may want some type of collateral or assurance that they will get their money back. It boils down to the evaluation of your business and proving that your business can make money and generate substantial profits. Also, most lending institutions and investors take other key factors into consideration when deciding whether or not to lend money to your new business.

<u>Key Factors for Business Stability:</u>
1   History of the company financial management and credit rating.
2   Evaluation of company's financial performance.
3   Company's ability to repay the loan.
4   Time frame in which company can repay the loan.

Let's take a closer look at each of the key factors for a better understanding of how to apply them and incorporate them into your company's processes and protocol.

A. **Financial Management-** is the involvement of all activities pertaining to money and how to best use it, whether it be for business or personal structure. True financial management consists of setting realistic goals and having the discipline to accomplish those goals. A good financial manager, not only understands the best ways to raise capital but also must be certain that the company stays within budget.

Chief Financial managers or CFO's make certain that capital is on the books and available for use when needed. CFO's must also make sure all debt is repaid efficiently in conjunction with getting the best and lowest interest rate. It is true that a financial manager can often be put in a catch 22 situation because the underlying problem is usually how to best use the funds to make the company more money. In the beginning, the ultimate dilemma is finding the investors or someone to finance your business. To figure out the type and amount of financing required will usually be based on the type of projects and activities that the company is currently engaged in or plan to do. Having a clear business plan with realistic and attainable goals will dictate the type and amount of financing you will need. Below is what I call the <u>Seven Principles of Proper Financial Management</u>. These principles have helped me succeed over the years. They help set the tone for your strategy and give you a blueprint on building your empire, or for those who may be rebuilding their empire.

<u>7 Principles of Proper Financial Management:</u>
1. Set company goals that are clear and realistic. To keep the capital flowing is the number one objective.
2. Be certain that all spending {ALL SPENDING} is discussed, planned and controlled by collectively by the CEO, CFO, and Board of Directors.
3. The highest priority is to make sure your business is adequately financed for the next five years. Or that funds and/or credit is available whenever needed.
4. Build and protect your company's credit and your personal credit as well. Pay your bills on time. You can't go to a well for water if the well is dry. ***Translation-how can you expect someone to trust you with their money if you've never kept your word and paid your bills on time?***
5. Keep a reserve account for emergencies and taxes only.

6. Collect on all account receivables. All lines of credit that you extend to customers should lag no more than thirty days. Any time after thirty days consider this account delinquent, and immediate action should be taken.
7. Develop a process and perfect it.

B. Evaluating a Company's Financial Performance: Other than dollars and cents, calculations and forecasts-how does a company evaluate its financial performance? Although there are many different methods, I'm going to share with you the four ways that I've found to be the most telling of the company and its management. These four methods are effective for preventing and identifying situations such as embezzlement, misappropriation of funds or goods.
-   Profit and Loss Statements (monthly, quarterly, semi-annually, and annually)
-   Cashflow analysis
-   Quarterly and annual audits
-   Inventory check-up once a month

C. Company's ability to repay debt. Other than a company's financial statement, a debt to income ratio is a good way to measure a company's financial strength. However, you should always take a look at current *sales* versus *expenses*. Also take a look at the company's sales forecast for the next five years. Rather you're selling a service, information or a product it's a good idea to do a speculative production forecast. A speculative production forecast is simply the time frame between the definite date of production and the date of when the goods are actually being sold. For example, let's take a look at a company like Samsung. When Samsung want to get prepared for the Christmas season to sell their flat screen TV's- they actually begin production around February or March. So, Samsung goes to a bank or some type of lending institution to negotiate short term financing to buy raw materials to build the TV's, cover lease space and warehousing, pay employees, to pay for advertising costs and to cover the cost of goods until the goods are actually sold to retailers around October of the same year. I bet you are probably wondering 'why would a company as big as Samsung need a loan?' Even though Samsung is a conglomerate, and they sell products to retailers and directly to the public via the internet all year long, typically during the first part of the year sales are slow and as a result sales revenue is down. Also, around this time expenses are usually higher-due to taxes, increased inventory, labor. So therefore, the company seeks short term financing to cover itself until the goods are shipped to the retailers and payment is received. It usually takes about thirty to sixty days after the product is shipped to collect payment from the retailers. The money collected from the retailers is called sales revenue. Sales revenue is what is used to repay the short-term financing. We have so much ground to cover and its exciting. Let's move on and discuss the types of financing available.

- 2 -
Types of Financing

There are two different categories of financing your business; short-term and long-term financing. In the beginning, while you are just starting out and building your business-you will more than likely need long term financing. Once you get going, there may come a time when you will need to secure short-term financing. I'm going to explain in detail how to use each category of financing, because although you require short term or long-term financing, there are several different methods of creative financing that can be applied within both categories.

For example, short-term financing is borrowed money; a loan that will be used by the company for one year or less. This type of financing is done usually to float the company's cashflow for a brief period of time. The repayment of the loan can be structured against future assets or sales. When a company requires long-term financing, it's usually because of expansion of products, services or facilities; purchase of new equipment; marketing and promotional campaigns or maybe the business is in need of funding for the next couple of years for sustainability. Long-term financing eases the strain of managing your day to day operations. But without proper accounting principles and superb money management skills your business may become a burden and you could end up filing for bankruptcy.

Since the economic meltdown of 2008-2009, lending institutions and investors as well, have been very selective on the types of loans available for businesses. This is largely due to the economy crawling to recover as well as government shut downs, along with tighter government regulations and political financial reform. So, where do you go to finance your existing business? Who do you ask to fund your new business? Other than conventional unsecured bank loans there are a multitude of methods a company can use to secure short-term financing.

Types of Short-term Financing

1. **Equity financing:** If your company is a corporation you can sell the common stock (shares) in a company to get capital. Or you can sell a set of special shares called preferred stock, in which case the lender or investor will loan the money in exchange for the preferred shares. The preferred shares are a form of collateral-special shares created to secure funding. Once the loan is paid back in full, the shares are then dissolved after an agreed upon period of time. Controllers/owners of the preferred shares must receive their dividend payments before the common stockholders receive their dividend payout.

2. **Bank or Credit Union backed by account receivables:** Account receivables are funds that are owed to a company that the customers haven't paid yet. Your business can use its account receivables as a form of collateral against a short-term loan. The lender may take some time to examine the financial stability of the company and may do a forecast analysis. Once the analysis is completed the

lender may advance the company a loan based on a negotiated percentage of the account receivables valuation.

3. **Account receivables sold to a Factor Firm:** A factor firm, also known as a factoring firm is a company that buys the accounts receivables of other companies. The factoring firm usually buys the accounts for a fraction of what the account is worth. Then the factor firm attempts to collect upon the full amount of the accounts. The firm makes a profit when it collects on the account receivables. It's a win for both parties; the company sold its account receivables for a lower price than the actual value of the account-but managed to get the short-term financing needed for the business. The factor firm won because this is their specialty-they've now assumed the risk of collections and can surely stand to make a large profit from the accounts.

4. **Trade Credit:** This is the most common type of short-term financing within the world of business. Typically, the manufacturer or wholesaler extends the trade credit to the retailer. In other words, the wholesaler doesn't need the cash right away, so they will ship the merchandise along with an invoice for the cost of goods. The wholesaler arranges a deal that allows the retailer to pay later-usually within thirty to sixty days. As long as the retailer keeps their commitment to pay their bill of extended credit-then the wholesaler will continue to grant more trade credit for the retailer to purchase more merchandise. A major key and benefit to using trade credit is that it's interest free financing.

5. **Promissory Notes and Commercial Paper:** These two tools are the final creative ways to generate capital by using a form of credit. But unless you are a large corporation such as Microsoft or Apple-it will be very difficult to get

someone to accept your short-term - promissory pledge
to pay. The same is true when writing commercial paper
because the only collateral is the reputation of the company.
But for your own knowledge-I'm going to explain the function and system of promissory notes and commercial paper.

5a. Promissory notes are a legally binding written contracts
that are enforceable in court. It is a written promise to
pay by the borrower (which is me or you) promising the
wholesaler or lender that we (our company) will pay
a particular dollar amount by a certain date. Since the
promissory note is a negotiable instrument the manufacturer, wholesaler or lender can sell the note to a bank
or another investor for a certain percentage of the note
to recoup their money.

5b. Commercial Paper is a form of a short-term promissory
note. Typically, commercial paper is only issued by
very large companies such as Winnebago, Ford, Microsoft, Coca-Cola and other corporate giants. When your
firm issues commercial paper, it will pay an interest
rate slightly lower than the banks' prime rate. Getting
someone to accept your commercial paper can be a
very daunting task, simply because you are not a large
enough company. Sometimes bigger is better.

Types of Long-term Financing

There are four types of long-term financing. We shall go
over each one individually for a better understanding and how
and when to utilize each one. The four types of long-term
financing are:

1. Equity Financing
2. Venture Capital Financing

3. Term Loan Financing
4. Private Placement

Each one of these methods are effective but the key is to figure out which one is best for your business. Let's begin with equity financing.

Since the financial crisis of 2008-2009, it has been very challenging to get long term conventional bank financing for those individuals and corporations with less than perfect credit. You can raise funds through the sale of shares. Or you can sale a negotiated interest of ownership by percentage, with all-inclusive rights to patents in exchange for funds-and after the expiration date or payoff of the loan-all rights revert back to the corporation.

Venture Capital Financing is rarely available to small businesses such as a car wash, clothing store, beauty salon, hardware store or barber shop. Unless these businesses have a chain of stores or the potential to franchise, venture capitalists tend to shy away from investing in them. Venture capitalists typically like to invest in innovative science, bio-tech, tech businesses or large companies that can produce a ROI of millions of dollars quickly. In most cases, the venture capitalists are a group of investors that are looking to share in your business profits and take part ownership in exchange for their cash, resources, risk, and contacts that they will utilize to make your business successful. You can easily search online for venture capitalist networks.

Term Loans: This type of loan is considered to be long term. In some cases, the loan repayment can be spread out over twenty years. Although it is typical that the loan is repaid within seven years. Quite often the lenders of the term loan will require some sort of collateral. So be well prepared to explain your plan and the reason why you and your company should get the funds.

Private Placement: When selling your corporate stock through a private placement-there is less government regulation. Therefore, the cost of doing business is less, along with minimal public scrutiny. The terms can be privately negotiated and swiftly executed.

Regardless of the path of financing that you choose for your business, always remember to be responsible, accountable, and honest. Being broke is only a temporary illness caused by a *poor* state of mind. You must take a risk in order to complete the journey. Never settle for less, always strive to achieve greatness. It is just as equally important to know that no matter how wealthy you are, at the end of the day, you can only do three things with money:
1. Spend it
2. Invest it
3. Or do nothing with it.

Sorry to disappoint you but when you die-you can't take your money with you. So, understand the purpose for money in your life. Put all things in proper perspective; God first, your health and safety, your family's health and safety, then your business and career. Also, one last piece of advice-never ever hire your brother, sister, cousin, or any other relative to do a job. You will surely regret it. It can destroy your relationship with them and possibly cripple your business. Never mix personal relationships with professional relationships-such as dating or sleeping with business partners and subordinate staff-it's a ticking time bomb just waiting to explode.

- 3 -
Breaking Down the Banking Industry

The Federal Reserve System is the key to controlling the power of the entire world. In order to fully understand business, you must be aware of a few things about banking and how the funds for loans originate and how interest rates work. But in order to understand that information-you need to know how the system function. That is the reason why we're going to begin by taking a look at the United States Federal Reserve System, also known as the FED. The Federal Reserve was created by congress in 1913 on December, 23rd for the purpose of effecting and regulating the United States banking system to ensure that the United States economy never falter and is always strong and vibrant.

The Federal Reserve is controlled by a 7-member team known as the Board of Governors. Each of the seven *are* and *must* be appointed by the President of the United States. Once they are appointed by the President, it is then up to the senate to confirm the appointee. The term of service for a board of governor's seat is fourteen years. The Federal Reserve System is comprised of 36 banks; 12 of those banks are district banks and the other 24 are called branch banks. All 36 banks are systematically scattered throughout the United States in various cities. The Federal Reserve, as a collective {its 36 banks and 7-member board} provide cashflow to banks to provide loans to you (to consumer and business owner), while simultaneously providing stability to our economy by controlling interest rates and inflation. In addition to controlling interest rates and infla-tion-The FED primary and unmistakable function is to regulate the United States overall supply of money. This is done by using a law called, 'the monetary policy'. The monetary policy is how the Federal Reserve decides the amount of money to supply to the nation and what interest rates should be charged. This is accomplished by controlling the bank reserve require-ments, regulating the discount rate and federal funds rate on all open market operations-i.e. stock markets, mutual funds, futures, commodities, and more.

So, here's how it works, the Federal Reserve loans money to the banks and then charge the bank a discounted rate or lower interest rate to pay back the money. Since the banks received a great rate, they turn around and offer lower rates to the public on mortgages, auto loans, business loans, credit cards, and personal loans. The incentive for the lower rates is to keep the money flowing- therefore stimulating the economy. Now when the Federal Reserve charges the banks a higher rate to borrow the money-that increase is also passed along onto you.

The Reserve Requirements can indirectly affect you and your business. Although it is rarely done, The Federal Reserve has the power to adjust the percentage requirement. When this happens the reserve requirement amount increases and the banks are then forced to retain more of the deposits, therefore they will have less money available for loans to the public. When fewer loans are made to the consumer-the money stops flowing and the economy becomes stagnant.

The Discount Rate-is the factor that affects how the
banks operate, what investors do with their money-which in
turn affects the health of the economy. For example, when
banks can borrow money from the Federal Reserve at a lower
discount rate then the process of loaning money to the public
becomes much easier because banks can extend loans to the
consumer and businesses at a lower interest rate, while still
making a significant profit and keeping the Nation's cashflow
flowing.

Although the control of the United States of America's
money circulation has much to do with the discounted rate,
the flow of money is largely affected by the Federal Open
Market Committee, whose primary function is to buy and sell
government securities such as treasury bills, treasury notes
and government bonds. The purpose of selling the government securities is to reduce the amount of money circulating
throughout the country. When an investor buys the securities from the government- the investors' money is then taken
completely out of circulation. The opposite is true when the
government want to increase the supply of money. They
simply buy back the government issued securities upon their
maturity date-of course with a little interest compounded, thus
increasing the supply of money that's in circulation throughout
the country. This process is called open market operations and
it can have an immediate and tremendous impact on not only
the United States economy but it can also impact the world's
economy.

The Federal Reserve System is the bank of the United
States and it is controlled by the World Bank. The World
Bank is an international financial institution that loans money
to countries. It has over 189 countries signed on as members.

The World Bank and its controlling committee are the supreme power over the Federal Reserve. Scary isn't it? No need to panic, we've been in this matrix for decades unwittingly. Do some research on the World Bank, Tri-Lateral Commission and Council of Foreign Relations.

Allow me to explain the Truth in Lending Act and how the Federal Reserve System enforces it. The Truth in Lending Act means that the lenders must make known to the borrowers what their annual interest rate, interest charges, pre-payment penalties, and other finance fees will be. The Truth in Lending Act was passed by Congress in 1968 for the purpose enforcing fair lending and ethical business practices. Other responsibilities include the clearing of checks and electronic funds transfers, income tax deposits, as well as the inspection and destruction of worn out currency and the application of selective credit controls. Selective credit controls are a percent margin set in place that outlines the parameters and amount of money that an investor must first put up to buy securities. That percent margin is usually set at 50%. In other words, if the investor requests to purchase the securities at fifty-thousand dollars, then the investor must come up with half of that amount-which is twenty-five thousand dollars.

There are different types of financial institutions that specialize or offer unique services.

The reason why different types of financial institutions offer different services is to prevent a monopoly of banks and businesses, because there is extreme competition for consumer business within the banking world. Let's take a closer look at each type of financial institution and their functions;

1. **Credit Unions** are the type of lending intuition that will only lend to its members. The members are usually

comprised of people living in the same demographics (county or city) or sometimes people that are in a similar profession and members of their family. There are close to 7,800 credit unions within the United States and they face strict regulations from the National Credit Union Administration and some state authorities as well. The benefit for joining a credit union is may be able to get a loan with mediocre credit simply because you're a responsible member, however at conventional commercial banks that may not be the case.

2. **National Banks and State Banks** are classified as commercial banking institutions and they are designed to turn a profit while offering a broad spectrum of product such; loans, checking and saving's accounts, bank credit cards, IRA's and safety deposit boxes. Banks are either federally chartered by the U.S. comptroller of currency-giving the bank permission to operate as a national bank-and as such the bank is subject to federal regulations. Or the lending insti-tution may be a state bank. A state bank can offer some similar services-but not all of the services as a national bank. Also, state banks are chartered by the State Banking Authorities, they are typically smaller in size and holdings and offer less products and services compared to National Banks. There are close to 1,500 national chartered banks in the United States and there's three times that amount of state banks. According to data compiled from fortune.com-2010 and research by Pride, Hughes Kapoor's-eleventh edition business book; there are seven major national banks in the United States. These banks are the largest and generate

the most revenues annually. They're listed below from largest to smallest based on the amount of revenue each generate annually and the total number of employees.

Bank Name	Revenue	Employees
Bank of America Corporation	150,450,000	283,717
J.P. Morgan Chase and Co.	115,632,000	222,316
Citigroup	108,785,000	267,150
Wells Fargo	98,636,000	267,300
Goldman Sachs Group	51,673,000	36,200
Morgan Stanley	31,515,000	61,388
American Express	26,730,000	58,300

These seven national banks offer full services and each one should be monitored very closely by the federal government. These banks have unlimited world power and influence beyond anyone's imagination. The products and services offered by each bank include but it not limited to; international banking, point of sale terminals, electronic transfer services, check clearing services, conventional loans, commercial loans, credit card services, and some may even offer financial advice.

3. **Savings and Loan Associations** also known as an S&L Corp, are financial institutions that provide checking, savings and CD accounts but primarily prefer to invest their assets into home mortgages, business loans and personal loans. There are close to 1,000 Savings and Loan Associations within the United States. Savings and Loan Associations are insured by the FDIC and therefore are subjected to state and federal regulation.

4. **Brokerage Firms** are financial institutions that are licensed to facilitate the buying and selling of securities. A brokerage firm usually represents a group of clients that are seeking to invest in public traded stocks, mutual funds, bond trades and other securities. Some brokerage firms offer margin loans to purchase stock. Edward Jones, Charles Schwab, Fidelity, TD Ameritrade would be classified as brokerage firms. These firms and their agents are a great source for investment information, goal setting and financial planning. They can help you start your portfolio.

5. **Finance Companies** are a great source of funding business and consumer loans. Typically, finance companies offer loans and extended credit to those that have marginal credit and to those who ordinarily qualify for a loan through a bank or conventional lending institution. You may have to pay a higher interest rate on the money borrowed but at least you will get the financing that you need.

I once heard a saying, "that Momma knows best". Well in the banking industry the FDIC and NCUA knows best. The FDIC was created because of the collapse of so many banks during the great depression in 1929. People lost their stock investments, homes were foreclosed, businesses went bankrupt, people lost all of their savings accounts that were in the banks. There was no recourse. It was a harsh and cruel time. Many people committed suicide from the pressure, embarrassment and anxiety of lost fortunes. So, to make certain that this catastrophe never happened again to the American people, congress passed a law that gave birth to the Federal Deposit

Insurance Corporation. The FDIC insures every account up
to a max amount of 250,000 dollars. Likewise, the National
Credit Union Association insures accounts of member credit
unions up to a max amount of 250,000 dollars as well. You can
get additional coverages for special or certain accounts. Speak
with your banker for clarity-given that each financial institution operates slightly different from one another. Now that
you have an understanding of how the United States banking
system work, lets discuss how you fit into the equation of business, banking and investing.

- 4 -
The Cash Flow

Assets are the key to winning in the money game. Acquire as much as you can as quick as possible, but with caution. Every deal isn't a good deal, and things aren't always as they seem. So slow things down so you don't have to pay later. Resources are the road to real wealth building. Cash, inventory, real estate and company equipment all have value. By using the power of leverage, you can see your dreams materialize into reality. Knowing how to read a balance sheet or cashflow statement is the single most critical piece to solving your money problems and kick starting your business into overdrive.

In my first book 'Open your mind before your business', we discussed where the money is and how to get your share. We also learned about corporate structures and how to properly set up your company. I gave you a tremendous amount of information on which business are best financially, easy to start and which ones are not so great. Now we are going into the next level. You have the business going, now it's time to discuss how to keep the cash flowing.

On my list of top four ways to keep the cash flowing, **non-profits** came in at **#1**. The golden rule is, to always give back to those less fortunate than you. If you do, I promise that you'll be blessed with ten times more than what you originally gave. Starting a non-profit organization requires time, commitment, dedication and transparency. To properly set up a non-profit consult a CPA. This is a great way to receive tax breaks and incentives, raise money or goods for a worthy cause, while simultaneously making a positive difference within the community. Goodwill, Boys and Girls Club, Girl Scouts of America, and Teen Challenge are all examples of nonprofit organizations. Although most nonprofits have plenty of volunteers as workers and helpers, as a director or employee of the nonprofit- the board of directors could vote to pay you a salary. Or provide you with things such as a company car, company gas card, or company credit card.

#2, - a Roth IRA is a great investment strategy for your retirement savings. The benefit to a Roth IRA is that the dollars you are putting into that account have already been taxed and therefore once you reach retirement and you want to withdraw the money, including all interest, there's a strong possibly all funds may be tax free. Also, Roth IRA's offer more options as well even before retiring, please see your financial advisor for more details.

There's no mistake about it, mutual funds have tremendous growth potential due largely in part to the earning power of the securities that are within the fund and that's why **Mutual Funds** are a strong **#3**. Although some mutual funds can be high risk which causes the dividend payment to vary from time to time, overall mutual funds are investments that can generate a good income for you. It's no secret that mutual funds can be converted into cash quickly if necessary. A mutual fund is when multiple investors pool their money together to invest in a variety of or group of several securities. If you choose to invest in mutual funds make sure you do your own research before you go to a brokerage firm to purchase. Or make an initial visit to a broker's agent and gather information and ideas on which funds are performing best for the past six months. Be sure to get the prospectus on those funds that you are interested in. Some of the most popular firms for buying and selling stocks and mutual funds are Schwab, Edward Jones, Merrill Lynch, Scot trade and E*TRADE, but there are so many more. I suggest you do your research on each company and their fees, then choose the companies that are going to best suit your goals.

There are several types or classifications of mutual funds that a person can invest in:

1. Growth stock fund
2. Index fund
3. High yield bond fund
4. Global stock fund
5. Aggressive growth stock fund
6. Income(corporate) stock fund
7. Sector stock fund

And the list goes on and on. There are a variety of mutual funds and the description of the fund indicates the type of securities that are within the fund. To find out the share value of a mutual fund – you will need to find out its net asset value. This is something you won't have to worry about because the net asset value is calculated once a day and is listed on the internet, newspapers and financial publications. You just need to know how to read and interpret the information. I simply want to point you in the right direction and spark ideas of aspiring entrepreneurs. Allow me to share some interesting facts of mutual fund investors in the United States, this data was compiled by State farm Investment company factbook from the years 2012 through 2014.

<u>United States Mutual Fund Investors</u>
Around 52.3 million households are vested in shares of mutual funds.
Of the 52.3 million mutual fund investors
42% are baby boomers' generation (born between 1946 and 1964)
 25% are generation X (my generation-born between 1965 and 1979)
16% are generation Y (born between 1980 and 1999)

So, take a look at the statistics and see which category you fall within. Learn what people from other demographics and social classes are doing. Do you own any assets? Mutual funds are a great way to start investing. For more information regarding which mutual funds are performing well you can contact several sources; Morning star Inc, Standard & Poor's, or Mergent's Investor Research Service. Also publicly held corporations must release reports of company's services, prod-ucts, financial statements and performance status. And I repeat, it doesn't hurt to have the company's prospectus available. For most people, this is just good information but it is useless until your actually apply it and start investing.

#4 on my list is a practical way to retire young and retire rich, if you know what you're doing or have a great team around you, then **Real Estate** is the way to go. My game plan is basic economics, so establish a budget of how much you can afford to spend on a property $70,000 - $90,000. Also figure out what type of properties that you want to buy; commercial or residential? Single family homes or apartments? Please know your niche and market before you make a move. It is a good idea to understand the demographics of the places your considering- low crime areas are a must. Knowing where you are buying is equally as important to knowing what you are buying. REO's is another source in real state that can produce decent investment income. REO is an acronym for the words real estate owned. These types of properties are bank owned. In most cases they have been foreclosed upon. Since the mortgage went into default, the bank now owns the property. Bankers are not in the business of owning real state. Some-times you can get some very good deals through REO's.

For Example:
The bank has a property that they are selling for $47,000
The property is valued at $65,000
The bank wants 20% down- so $9,400, along with good credit will get you the property.
Minor upgrades and property rehab should cost $10,000. Your total vested amount after all upgrades is $47,600. At that point have the property appraised again and put it on the market for sale.
Sell it for $70,000
Deduct your expenses of $47,600.00

That's a profit of $22,400.00. Not every deal is going to be as lucrative as my example, but some will. You have to take your time and focus on buying the right kind of properties. I also buy distressed properties if they are in a low crime- middle class area. These properties bring in a positive cash flow almost always. Sure, you can flip properties the way I showed you with the REO's but the goal in real estate is long term investing and continuous cash flow. Therefore, you may want to consider keeping most of your properties and here's why:

Imagine you purchased a distressed property from the city for $20,000 dollars cash- no mortgage. You spend another $20,000 dollars rehabbing the property. So now your total debt/money invested is $40,000 dollars. Once the property is back up to code and in livable conditions, you have an appraiser come out to assess the property at $75,000 dollars. Since you don't have a lien on the property it is considered to be a free and clear asset. Most lending intuitions are willing to loan up to 80% of the appraised value. Multiply .80 by $75,000 dollars (the appraised value) and it equals $60,000 dollars. The lender will place a lien/ mortgage on your property for $60,000 dollars and give you a check for that amount when you close on the deal. Deduct your expenses of $40,000 and you will have a cash difference of $20,000 dollars. You just made $20,000 dollars on your property and you still get to keep it. Let's assume that your mortgage, taxes, and insurances is around $400 hundred dollars per month and you rent the prop-erty to someone for $900.00 per month. So, if you acquire ten, twenty, or thirty properties netting a positive cashflow profit of a minimum $500.00 each property per month imagine the possibilities of success.

Let's do the math: 500.00 per month x 12 months x 30 proper-ties = $180,000 dollars annually.

The beauty of real estate is that it can appreciate (go up in value) at the same time it depreciates (goes down in value). Which means that the IRS/ government allow us to deduct a certain dollar amount off of our taxes each year. The appreciation/depreciation formula creates a profit for you called a capital gain. When this happens, you've just made money again. Capital gains are often taxed around forty percent of the gross income. See your accountant for your city and state's tax code.

Most people don't know that you can never own real estate. You can only 'control' it. The reason that you can never own it is because it belongs to the government. The word real originated from the Latin root word 'res' – meaning real. The Latin word 'rex' means royal and these two words together refers to medieval kings and queens owning all of the land in their kingdoms and the citizens had to pay a tax on the land to reside there or to farm on it. Similar to what we do today with property, hence the reason why we pay property taxes on our properties each year. Think about it, you own your shirt but you don't have to pay taxes on it continuously. You can own a coat, purse, jewelry, weapons, even motorcycles and boats- yet we never have to pay taxes on any of those things continuously. Now that we established how to benefit from controlling property, I'd like to share with you some idea's that may help you decide what type of real estate to invest in.

Types of Real Estate:
1. Commercial Property- which are business suites, offices and small retail stores
2. Commercial Retail – which are Large retail storefronts sitting on several acres of land like Lowe's
3. Industrial Property- which are like plants such as GM, or prisons, and all manufacturing companies.

4.   Multi-family units- which are apartment units
5.   Warehouse facilities
6.   Vacant plots of land
7.   Single family homes.

Regardless what you decide to invest in, I encourage you
to learn your craft and never be afraid of a challenge. Just
remember when investing in real estate there are always four
main things to consider; location, condition of property, price,
and terms. You don't have to be a sophisticated or savvy
investor to do the things that I've shared. You simply need to
be MOTIVATED. A good understanding of business is helpful,
along with a typed-well thought out plan of how you are going
to accomplish your goals. The main objective is to get out
of the rat race of working a job that consumes most of your
time. Please do not rely on your job as security and comfort.
The money you make from your job is earned income, which
means that it is taxed at a higher rate and it is barely enough
to get by on now. Without solid investments, surely retirement will bring most people financial hardship and regret.
The alternative is to convert your hard work into hard cash by
doing less manual labor and more self-empowering by opening
businesses, investing in mutual funds, stocks, bonds, and
controlling real estate for profit. These are the things that will
allow us to be financially free.

There are many products to invest in, but just as you
created a plan for your business, you'll also need a solid
plan before you invest. We must get rid of all of those silly
quotes and comical cliché's and throw them right out of the
window. Cliché's such as 'scared money doesn't make
money'. First off, money isn't a living creature, therefore it

can't feel an emotion of love or fear. Or how about this one, 'money makes the world go around'. That's not true either, money doesn't make the world go around, gravity does. I believe that small businesses and good commerce make the economy boom. Here's the ultimate cliché; 'it takes money to make money'. That's also false. It takes brains to create real wealth. Everyone can't do it. Some people may have heard 'it's all about the Benjamin's'. Well I believe, 'it's all about the businesses. The Benjamin's will come as long as my business skills are solid, my level of understanding is clear, my goals are clear and written down, the numbers are right, the business proposal is impeccable and it seems like a good deal for my team. So, you see, it's all about the business. I showed you, in my first book, how you can make money even if you don't have any money to begin with. Dispel those silly clichés', those sayings were created for broke people by broke people. In order to arrive and sustain at the level of financial stability you must change your way of thinking. Have you ever heard of the saying, 'you are what you eat'? Well I believe, 'you are what you think.' Below is a list of investments, their risk level and rate of return.

Investment Type	Risk Level	Rate of Return
Bank Account of any form	Low	Low
Mutual Funds	Moderate	Moderate, Sometimes high returns
Real Estate	Moderate	High returns
Government Bonds	Low	Low returns
Stock Options	High	High returns
Precious Metals/ Commodities	High	High returns
Broker firm (Trade paper debt for cash)	High	High
Coins & Antiques	High	Moderate
Jewels, Precious Stones	High	High
Bio/ Tech Companies	High	High

- 5 -
Your Retirement Plan

It is never too early to start planning for your retirement years. And its never too late to consider your options, even if you haven't been saving and planning. Regardless of your age and what point you are at in life- rather you are just entering the workforce or you've been in your chosen career for quite some time- it's imperative that you have a plan for your retirement. The sooner you start planning the better off your life will be upon retirement. So, what do you plan on doing when you're sixty-five or seventy years old? Do you have a vision? Can you picture yourself living at that age? And if so, what will you live off of?

We are going to discuss five different plans and hopefully you can get an idea of which plan is best for you based on your age and the IRS guidelines. Before we begin, please understand that this is a long-term investment program. Retirement investment is a strategy designed within a measurable and reasonable amount of time tailored to your personal needs, while taking into consideration your financial strengths and weaknesses. In order to accomplish the strategy of long-term investing three things must happen;

1. You must set realistic goals based on the current economy
2. You must figure out how much money you want to invest every month
3. You should start small and grow your investment portfolio as you gain experience. Give yourself a specified time frame; ten, twenty- and thirty-year increments, of how much money you want saved in your retirement account.

The first type of retirement plan that we are going to discuss is the pension fund. The pension fund is set up by your employer. Typically, this type of fund invests in corporate stock, government bonds, and government securities. Or sometimes they will invest in low risk mutual funds. The purpose of the pension fund is to guarantee the employee a monthly income once he or she retire from the company. Both the employee and the employer can contribute to the fund.

The second type of retirement plan is probably the most popular, it is known as the 401k and it was established for profit earning companies. With this type of retirement plan you (the employee) can contribute a certain maximum allowed dollar amount and the company will contribute a certain percentage or match your contribution dollar for dollar. This type of investment is subject to tax penalties for early withdrawal. Be sure to sit with your company HR department to decide if this is the best move for you.

The third type of investment retirement plan is the 403b. It is very similar to the 401k, except that the 403b was established for government agencies and non-profit corporations.

Like the 401k the 403b is subject to tax penalties upon early withdrawal.

Our fourth type of retirement investment plan is one that offers tax deductible incentives; which means that the money you deposit into the account is not taxed until you withdraw it years later. This type of retirement plan is the known as the traditional IRA. IRA is an acronym for Individual Retirement Arrangement/Account. Let's assume that you earn 50,000 dollars per year at your job. You decide to move 5,000 dollars into your IRA. When you file taxes, you would only file on the 45,000 dollars as taxable income. The other 5,000 will remain in the IRA and accumulate for years to come. You cannot withdraw the money from the IRA until age 59. If you withdraw the money before age 59, you will be subjected to pay income tax and an early withdrawal fee of ten percent of the withdrawal amount. There are two types of IRA's; personal or business. If you are a business owner, a business IRA is something you may want to consider.

The fifth and final retirement investment plan is the Roth IRA. Unlike the traditional IRA, a Roth IRA contribution is not tax deductible. For example; if you earned 50,000 dollars for the year and you want to contribute 5,000 dollars to your Roth IRA, you'd still be taxed (now) on the entire 50,000 dollars. But one major benefit is that when you withdraw the money from your Roth IRA- none of the money is taxed- including all earnings- as long as your account has been open for more than five tax years. To start a personal traditional IRA account, you will need a minimum of 500 dollars. For a Business IRA account, you will need a minimum of 2,000 to 3,000 dollars. Below is a comparison chart of the Roth versus the Traditional IRA.

Roth IRA	Traditional IRA
Can withdraw 10,000 in profits for 1st time home buyer expenses.	Penalized for early withdrawal
Contributions aren't tax deductible	Can get a tax break on contributions made from earned income (job)
Great vehicle for long term wealth building	Great for immediate tax incentives
Easier to pass money to heirs	Tax deferred – essentially tax breaks equate to savings

** See your banker for more details, as each state may have different banking regulations.

- 6 -
Franchising

Planet Fitness, 7-11, McDonalds, Burger King, C-21 Realty Company, Merry Maids, Tuffy Muffler, Dairy Queen, Ford, Nissan, Dodge, or Chevrolet- are all examples of franchises. Franchises are very lucrative and employ thousands of people. Everyday people depend on the product or services of these franchises. They're in high demand and they're the real corporate giants. But they didn't start out that way. Every one of those companies that I named started out with one location, one brand, and hardly any money.

Franchising started in the mid 1800's during the civil war as a way for huge companies to sell and expand their product and brand. Around the 1900's the automobile industry- lead by Henry Ford- saw that franchising as an economical way of distributing his companies' automobiles, as such car dealerships sprung up everywhere, along with manufacturing companies and full-service gas stations. It didn't take long for the fast food industry to transform itself and jump on the band wagon and by the 1970's fast food franchisees were experiencing tremendous growth, development and profits.

The 1970's brought about free spirits, radicalism, and individuality, all of which increased the popularity of franchises.

Today, in this new millennium- it appears that franchising is the future and has expanded into global domination; i.e. McDonald's is in China, Burger King is in London, England, and KFC is in Germany. There is strength in numbers as I will explain how the pieces fit together. A franchise happens when a business grants a license to an individual, group or company to operate, advertise and to do business under the business name and brand, while functioning as a part of a chain of outlets. The one granting the license is called the franchisor. The one purchasing the franchise or receiving the license is the franchisee. The franchisor supplies the business name, reputation, brand, proven management process, proper training, promotional materials and a successful process for doing business. The franchisee role is polar opposite, as they are totally hands' on, running the day to day operations by providing; labor and money (working capital). The franchisee must agree to follow all of the guidelines of the franchise agreement or jeopardize their business by breach of contract.

There are three different strategies that can be used for forming a franchise;

#1. You can facilitate a license agreement, whereas you would license a distribution company to sell your products to retailers. This strategy is routine business within the alcohol, coffee, and tobacco industries.

#2. The Franchisor owns the real estate and the building – and you pay a monthly rent for the space and facilities to operate. The franchisor will provide the portal to purchase supplies- that you will be responsible to pay for. The franchisor will also provide the brand, reputation, distribution, and network of support. You

can probably negotiate royalty percentages. This is a
simple form of franchising. Personally, I don't like this
method because I believe that it takes advantage of the
little guy.

#3. The third strategy is when you own the property and
lease the property to yourself, while using the franchisors product, brand, and reputation to operate under and
through a license agreement. The majority of new car
dealer dealerships are set up this way.

The majority of franchises are successful when growth
and development are controlled. Also, when there is a strong
support team in place for the franchisee, the team seems more
motivated to want to make the business succeed. It is equally
important to have an efficient process in place. You'll want to
have a smooth process- from the greeting to the purchase, no
pressure – just subtle suggestions. However, I caution you;
if you like doing things your way, you don't like to listen to
counsel or advice, you have a hot temper, or you don't like to
follow instructions or directions- then being a franchisee may
not be for you. I've listed some things that you can expect
when you enter a franchise agreement. The franchisee (you)
will:

- pay a franchise fee and a royalty fee to the franchisor
- operate business hours according to the franchisor
- use the promotional items that franchisor chooses
- design the building, decorate and be in uniform
  according to franchisor
- purchase all product from the franchisor or vendor that
  franchisor select

- use the accounting software and sales platform that franchisor select
- use the trademarks, copyrighted materials, patents, and secret recipes as directed by franchisor

You have very little freedom to run your business the way you see fit when you are under a franchise agreement. It is pretty much the franchisors way or the highway. But if you follow the system you will reap huge rewards. You will be paid generously.

As a franchise operator you will work 12-hour days sometimes 7 days a week. Operating and being vested in a franchise may require you to do less of what you love or want and more of what you must do for the survival of the business. Also consider this, if you want to grow your empire, then you're going to need time- and that's the best asset that you can ever have.

Preparing and Understanding Financial Statements

When it comes down to money and business accountability, there's nothing more important or up close and personal than a company's financial statements. Bankers and investors rely on three statements for a pulse of how a business is doing financially. Think of an audit or deeper look into a company's financial statements as an x-ray, MRI, or blood test being performed on the business. The financial statements will not only tell us if something is wrong with the health of our business but also where the problem is located.

There are three different types of financial statements. I will list them below and then explain the function of each.

#1. Let's begin with the balance sheet. A balance sheet is a statement of financial position. The balance sheet gives a sum total of a company's assets, liabilities, and owner's equity for a particular time frame. A balance sheet can also be done on your personal finances as well. Think of your business as (your body). Now think of the company's financial strength as the health of the business(body). When we need to know the

health status of the company, we perform an audit-
which gives us the balance sheet. Below is an example
of a balance sheet:

<u>Balance Sheet</u>

Roland's Metal Factory Inc.   October 16, 20xx

<u>Assets</u>

Current Assets

Cash		69,000	
Marketable Securities	48,000		
Accounts Receivable	40,000		
Less Allowance for	2,000	38,000	
Negative accounts			
Receivables		25,000	
Merchandise Inventory	49,000		
Prepaid Expenses		2,000	
Total Current Assets			231,000

Fixed Assets

Production Equipment	175,500		
Less-Depreciation	25,300	152,200	
Furniture and Warehouse Equip.	85,000		
Less Accumulated Depreciation	15,000	70,000	
Total Fixed Assets			220,200

Intangible Assets

Patents		9,500	
Copy Rights		7,100	16,600
Trade Marks			
Total Assets			467,800

<u>**Liabilities and Stockholders' Equity**</u>
Current Liabilities

Accounts Payable	35,000		
Notes Payable	18,900		
Salaries Payable	3,700		
Taxes Payable	7,200		
Total Current Liabilities			64,800

Long Term Labilities

Mortgage Payable on Production Equip.	36,000		
Total Long-Term Liabilities		36,000	
TOTAL LIABILITIES			100,800

Stockholder Equity

Common Stock (50,000x4)		260,000	
Retained Earnings		107,000	
TOTAL OWNERS EQUITY			367,000
TOTAL LIABILITIES and OWNERS EQUITY			467,800

The formula is simple math; The assets must be equal to the liabilities plus owner's equity. There are many software programs such as QuickBooks and turbo tax solutions that can easily assist you with company accounting. The reason that I gave an example of a balance sheet is because I want you to familiarize yourself with the structure, so you will know what to look for when analyzing a balance sheet. Take a look under the assets section of the balance sheet- under this section, please be sure to list your most liquid assets first. Your most liquid assets are the assets that you can easily convert into cash if needed. Next list all marketable securities such as stocks, bonds, and mutual funds. Following the marketable securities, list all accounts receivables and current inventory. These items are all a part of the value of the company and can create cash-flow. If you notice, the two grand totals at the bottom of the balance sheet- assets 467,800 is the same as the liabilities plus owner's equity.

Enron, WorldCom, Lehman Brothers, AIG, General Motors, Fannie Mae, Bank of America and many more were all accounting disasters. These companies should be examples of how greed can destroy everything you ever worked for! Proper financial statements are crucial to the success of your business because a reflection of your record keeping, managing and budgeting are silently described within those three financial statements.

2. The Income Statement.

The income statement summarizes a company's revenues and expenses for a certain accounting period- rather monthly, quarterly, semi-annually, or annually. The income statement reflects the profit and loss dollar amount of a company. Rather your providing a product or service – every company's busi-ness is the business of sales. Sales are the driving force and support structure of every business. In order to truly know if a company is earning or losing money, perform an audit. The results from the audit is the information that is provided on the income statement. The income statement will clearly define a company's financial health and it will also centralize the area or areas where there may be a problem.

On the next page there is a sample income statement. I'll explain the statement and what you should be looking for when examining an income statement.

<u>Income Statement</u>

Roland's Metal Factory Inc.   October 16, 20xx

<u>Revenues</u>

Gross Sales	---	300,000	
Less Returns/Allowances	7,000		
Less Sales Discount	3,000	10,000	
Net Sales	---		310,000
Cost of Goods Sold	---	---	---
Beginning Inventory (01/01/20xx)	---	99,000	---
Purchases	219,000	---	---
Less Purchase Discount	10,000		
Net Purchases	---	209,000	
Cost of Goods Available For Sale		215,000	
Less Ending Inventory (12/31/20xx)		51,000	
Cost of Goods			164,000
Gross Profit	---	---	146,000
Operating Expenses	Overhead/ marketing	43,000	
Net Income before Taxes	---	---	103,000

Most income statements are comprised of four main sections; revenue, cost of goods sold, operating expenses, net income. Each main section can also have several subsections; such as under operating expenses you could actually list and itemize what each of the expenses are- rent, utilities, marketing and so on.

The Revenue Section is the pre-tax dollars earned by the company. You should always begin by listing your gross sales-which are the total dollars of all goods and services minus returns, sales allowances, and sale discounts. The difference between the revenue and gross sales is the company net sales and that number is to be listed to the right.

Cost of Goods Section- there is a very simple formula that's used when computing the cost of goods sold by a company;

Cost of Goods sold= beginning inventory + purchases- ending inventory.   Cost of goods must include everything you purchase to make that item/ service complete and salable. You must include cost for raw materials, screws, and labor. If you remember from my first book, "Open your mind before your business", I said always keep a great team of professionals around you. Even with a team of professionals around you, you still need to know how to read these statements and know what to look for if there is a problem.

Operating expenses- is usually broke down into two sub sections; general expenses and selling expenses. General expenses are the costs for running your business such as sala- ries, utilities, internet, insurances and rent. Whereas selling expenses are promotional items, advertising costs, and anything related to the marketing arm of your business. If it costs you- list it. Add up the general and the selling expenses together for the total operating expenses and list that number to the right.

Net Income Section. To arrive at the net income simply subtract operating expenses from your gross profit. The formula is; Gross profit- total operating expenses = Net Income before taxes. Then you must deduct your taxable federal amount to arrive at your Net Income after taxes.

A Cash Flow statement tells all about your business. The sole purpose of a cash flow statement is to know how much cash a business has on hand. This is how you will know if a company can pay its bills, can determine if the business is in a position to expand or are, we about to close our doors and go out of business. Your accountant can create a cash flow statement for you by simply using the numbers provided on the balance sheet and the income statements. I am providing a great spring board for you to succeed in the realm of investing. I wish you the best of luck.

- 8 -
Integrity

Before I started writing this chapter, I considered talking about the importance of credit and credit management. But then I realized that we needed to discuss something far more important- Integrity. In fact, if you have integrity it should be a breeze for you to have proper credit management skills. So, what is integrity? And how do we get it? According to Merriam-Webster dictionary, 'integrity is the adherence of moral and ethical principles; soundness of moral character; honesty; the state of being whole, entire or undiminished.' In other words, integrity is a trait or quality that describes the positive actions and honesty of a person's character, beliefs, and attitude. You can't buy integrity, nor honesty. These are rare gifts that very few people possess now days.

Your word is all that you have. Even after all of the fame, the glitz, money, influence and power, only one thing will remain. When all of our superficial layers are peeled away and we are exposed for who we are, only one simple word will give testament to our character. Integrity! Over the years, I've watched family and former friends settle for the easy way out, or the fast dollar and the quick hustle. Every single time they've chosen to do a shady deal or break the law to make a dollar, it's ironic how they always end with more problems and they're still no further ahead.

Here's the deal, we can point fingers and never accept your faults. Or, you can choose to fight and build up the psyche of your moral compass. Positivity is contagious. Happiness is addictive, laughter is fun, and a peace of mind is like possessing a rare jewel. But you will never fully experience any of those blessing's until you humble your heart, change your current set of friends, remove yourself from the environment that's hindering your progress. Now is the time to focus your thoughts on building integrity. Building integrity is more spiritual than mental. The path to building integrity is a bumpy road, filled with solitude once you are able to tap into your spiritual energy. But just as intense heat is applied to create a beautiful diamond, we must endure the process of intense heat, shaping and molding our mind, body and spirit to become that rare jewel called integrity. A tree is only as strong as its roots. If the roots aren't durable and sturdy it will never grow strong. Unless you alter its genetics, its very existence. Well Its time for us to alter our very existence by immersing ourselves into the Word of God. We have to change our thought process and become spiritually stronger through prayer and fasting. We are going to destroy those negative thoughts of *depression, rage, suicide,* and *self-hate.* Those are all demons that can be destroyed through the power of the LORD. We are building ethics and changing our behaviors with vigor.

Causes of unethical behaviors:
1. **Individual Pressures-** personal goals not in agreement with the company/ business agenda. Or too much insider, sensitive information about a particular issue.

Or perhaps not enough knowledge and experience to handle certain situations. I remember when my grandmother used to always say 'if it feels wrong, then it probably is wrong, so don't do it.'

2. **Social Pressures-** when we are more concerned with how other people view us- is when we make poor decisions. Such influences are our level of tolerance for what we view as acceptable behaviors. Opinions of close friends and significant others affect how we behave or respond to life's most challenging situations. Other social pressures come from the exposure of bad information or immoral behaviors over the internet through various platforms.

3. **Insecurities/ low self-esteem-** When someone is insecure it is usually something that can be seen, unlike a thought. For example, an obese person walks into a room and the people in the room are whispering among themselves. No one knows what the people are whispering about but the obese person assumes that they are talking about him/ or her being overweight. Low self-esteem is largely due to the lack of confidence in yourself and caring too much about what others think of you. There are other insecurities as well; such as uneven skin complexion, excessive acne, body odor, worn out clothing or shoes, poor hygiene, crooked teeth, bad breath, too short, too skinny and the list goes on. It's very easy for people to criticize or even give advice on how to build up self-esteem. But until you've walked a mile in that other person's shoes, watch what you say and how you say it. It is difficult to seek counsel from anyone unless they've been in your situation before. A

text book and therapeutic training only goes so far. The
first step to correcting this behavior- is learning to love
yourself and being okay with who you are.

4. **Greed-** There is a war going on that we cannot see
but we are in the middle of it. That war is over human
souls. Good versus evil. God destroying Lucifer.
Greed has been the author of confusion since the beginning of time. The thirst of greed creates an ever-burning
desire to fill in an insatiable appetite of money, power,
notoriety, praise and material worldly possessions. I
remember back in the summer of 2005, when I was
selling cars at a Ford dealership in Michigan, I was just
trying to make an honest living and earn my place in
the world. Well, one day my cousin Larry called me
and said that he wanted a job. So, I arranged an inter-
view for Larry to meet the manager. The manager was
reluctant to hire my cousin but as a favor to me, the
manager hired Larry.
As I walked Larry to his car, I congratulated him on the
new job. I casually said, "Now you can get out of the
streets and stop selling dope."
With a puzzled look on his face he replied, "why would
I do that? I make more money than people that work at
General Motors. I ain't never gonna stop hustling."
Larry hugged me and jumped in his new truck and
headed down the road. As I slowly watched his truck
fade into the distance, I knew that was going to be
the last time that I saw my cousin alive. And it was.
About a week later police found him in his car- shot
in the head in a dark alley in Detroit. It was Larry's
greed that led to his untimely demise. Getting things

right now isn't always the best or safest way. Sometimes you have to sit down and be patient. Exercise critical thinking. Look for a better solution. But most important, pray to God for guidance and wisdom.

5. **Sexual Passion-** We are all tempted by lust. In fact, most of us make sex the centerpiece of our lives. For the passion that drives our desire to fornicate is the very thing that can quickly lead to a painful chastisement. Imagine going home to tell your spouse that you lost your job because you were sexually harassing young female staff members. Prostitution, rape, orgies, threesomes, porn, strip clubs, cheating on your wife, cheating on your husband, bunny ranches, any type of sex before marriage including gay and lesbian experimentations- are all sexual demons and the lust will drive you insane and to your demise if you're not prayed up with the total body armor of God.

6. **Conflict of Interest-** remember our ole buddy greed? Well greed is the agitator that appeals to our self-gain inclinations or feelings rooted deep within our minds. In other words, our instincts to survive can sometimes cause us to make irrational decisions. Moving along, when you put your personal gain and interest before the company, customer, product, and service that you are providing a conflict of interest will occur. Also, when gifts, tax free payments or extra percentages become apart of a business deal but is done off the books or under the table- most would look at that as a bribe. But the motivator behind the conflict of interest is greed.

7. **Lack of Proper Communication/Improper communication-** In other words, lying. Lies, lies, lies. Humans

have been lying since the beginning of time. And if
you think that I'm lying then read the book of Genesis
in the Holy Bible.   Sometimes we lie and don't even
know why we are lying. Lies have gotten innocent
people imprisoned, even murdered. In the business
world will only tarnish your image- but you will lose
your customer base and no one will respect you. Lying
will surely jeopardize your business and career. False
advertising or misleading information is unethical and
could result in harsh penalties such as loss of licenses,
fines, and in some cases jail time. As an example, take
a look at Bernard Madoff former Nasdaq chairman that
was convicted for being involved in the Ponzi scheme
of 2009. Or perhaps you are familiar with the mess that
was created by Enron or even WorldCom. All three
were examples of business executives operating out
of greed, telling lies to cover up their deception. Just
be honest with your customer, business associates and
yourself. It sure beats the embarrassment from being
exposed as a liar.

Let's clear the air in regards to business professionals that
have been labeled as whistle blowers- or snitches. The word
snitch (also known as a rat) is a slang term used on the streets
by people that are involved in the street life activities; criminals committing crimes. A snitch is someone that reports to
law enforcement or one that testifies in the court of law against
other criminals, usually the snitch's former partners in crime.
A snitch makes a deal to squeal to save their own behind. But
a whistle blower is different. A whistle blower is one that
informs the media, company officials and government agen-

cies of illegal or unethical methods taking place at the place of business within the scope of doing consistent business. A whistle blower is not a snitch, instead it is a person who has integrity and refuse to go along with the corrupt and deceitful activity within the company. Their ethics won't allow them to have a clean conscious and partake in wrong doing. Whereas a snitch was a snake to begin with. There wouldn't be anything to blow a whistle on if everyone had good moral character and was actually trying to live a Godly, righteous life. So, let's stop condemning and start clapping! I applaud Sherron S. Watkins for blowing the whistle on Enron. I commend Cynthia Cooper formerly of WorldCom, Jeffrey Wiest former accounts payable manager at Tyco Electronics. Great job for having the guts to go against the grain and stand up for what is right. It boils down to one word, integrity. So, lets change our thoughts and surely, we will change our lives.

I've listed a few examples of how far greed will get you. Kwame Kilpatrick former mayor of Detroit; Bernie Madoff- he's probably the most famous because of the amount of money involved; Keith Anderson, Wayne Anderson and Richard Marks of Anderson, Ark and Associates; and former CEO of Tyco Electronics Dennis Kozlowski. All of these men charged and convicted of federal crimes. You can call it misappropriation of funds, embezzlement, earning's manipulation, falsifying security and exchange reports- it doesn't matter. It still boils down to greed. So, think ethics, stay humble and you will rise to the top.

- 9 -
The Honey Bee Syndrome

Have you ever observed a bee hive? At first it appeared that the queen bee controlled the rest of the bees within the colony. As the other bees' scurry about collecting and spreading pollen, buzzing about working vigorously, the queen bee stays in the hive to lay eggs and attend to the young. The queen is to never leave the hive; the other bees feed her. She is well protected and heavily insulated deep within the hive. 'Wow, what a life!', was my first thought. But then I took a second look at things- from a different, clearer prospective.

When I took a second look, from my prospective the queen bee was not in control. She's a slave to her own society, held captive, forced to constantly reproduce and nurture the young warriors. She has the title of authority and gives the impression of having a position of power. But she works herself to death- literally- while her society benefits from her hard work and sacrifice. Upon death, the queen is tossed to the side and replaced by another with casual ease, never to be honored, recognized or remembered for all of her years of dedicated service. This is what I call the honey bee syndrome.

Does this story sound familiar to you? It should. Because the queen bee is every one of us that are trapped in a job that

we don't like or a career that is too time consuming or very
stressful. If you are not already wealthy and you are not doing
anything productive towards gaining your financial freedom-
then you are a slave to the system. You are a slave to a system
that you want to escape from but don't know how, so you stay
and work exuberantly until your death because of the company
benefits and consistent paychecks make you feel well protected
and heavily insulated. Then the joys and pressures of family
come about, as we nurture our young- preparing them to be
conquerors- leaders of the world. We work until our death,
trapped in the matrix, without any accolades or recognition
while we are alive. Under appreciated for our gifts, talent
and loyalty. And just like the queen bee, we are tossed aside
(in a casket) and replaced by another. Welcome to the honey
bee syndrome! It's an illusion created to make you think that
you have the power because you have the title. You've been
trapped in it your entire life, you just never knew that you
were in the syndrome, so therefore the likelihood of escape
is almost impossible. The nature of the system is designed to
induce complete psychological subjectivity thereby- allowing
complete population control. That is why, chances are if you
were born into a poor or middle-class family, that is where you
will remain for the rest of your life-unless, of course, if you're
an exceptional athlete, entertainer, singer or some tremendous
talent of the arts. Remember this- 'the skills and secrets of the
rich are never passed onto the poor.' The worker bee (the rich
and wealthy) need to continue the cycle of labor and toil with
the queen bee (you and I- the real workers) in order for them
(the rich and wealthy) to continue to prosper.

The rich and wealthy are labeled worker bees because
they are the ones in society building businesses, buzzing about

investing and selling, amassing wealth- spreading nectar to other rich and wealthy flowers.

You are the queen bee because you have the title of authority such as; manager or supervisor but your duties are menial and entry level or tedious and tiresome. You are on the ground working- trapped in an office and forced to produce dollar after dollar, sale after sale- all for the good of your hive (society, - the rich and wealthy). Meanwhile, you barely have enough money to put food on the table and pay your bills. This is the way in the honey bee syndrome. But today, I am going to share some information with you that can get you completely out of the honey bee syndrome and on your way to building wealth and power. Consider this; Bill Gates, George Soros, Paul Allen, Warren Buffett, Jeff Bezos, and Mark Zuckerberg are among the top ten wealthiest people in the entire planet. Combined, these five men have more money than 85% of the people on the earth. The motivation is for you get your share, and socialism doesn't work. You need to learn the secrets of capitalism and you need to know the movers and shakers of your vision. You may not make it to Bill Gates' level, but how will you know if you don't try.

Today you are going to change your future because today we are going to plan for the future and break the curse of the honey bee syndrome. We are going to take control by answering 8 important questions. Be honest with yourself, think long and hard. Now ask yourself:

1. What business will I start?
2. Why am I starting this business?
3. What skills will I need to make my business a success?
4. Who will assist me with my daily operations?

5. List 7 things that you love to do?
6. List 6 things that you hate to do?
7. How much money do you want to be worth in 5 years?
8. What is your mission, your #1 driving force for your life and business?

Once you can write the answers out to those 8 questions, you've just unlocked the number one hindrance of anyone becoming successful- YOUR MIND. Once you have unlocked the chambers of your mind the rest is smooth sailing. But you will need a strong team around you too. Beginning wealth builders should never spread their money too thin by diversifying. Initially, don't put all of your eggs in one basket either. The smart move is to use some for saving's in case of a rainy day, then create your first investment and watch it closely. As your investment grow, continue to cultivate it and then start another investment. Successful people only use credit to make more money. Successful people also build winning teams around them.

<u>Your Successful Team:</u>
1. Banker (full Service national bank)
2. Real Estate Broker
3. Corporate Attorney
4. Tax Attorney
5. Real Estate Attorney
6. Insurance Broker
7. Accountant
8. Discount Stock Broker.

This is your team of professionals. As time progress and

you grow in money and power you will know when to add each professional to the team.

The honey bee syndrome gives us nothing for a challenge. In fact, we become so complacent and lackadaisical that we no longer have a desire to be free. We simply accept our fate for what it is. We give up trying and become drone-like and robotic. Poor, hopeless, and miserable are the traits to describe such a person. You don't want to end up like that.

Most financial planners consider themselves experts with managing money. However, I believe that their method of doing things are a bit dated. We need something refreshing and invigorating, new methods, new investments. I went to see a financial planner once and his advice to me was keep my job and don't start a business, or even go after a better paying job, pay all of my bills every month on time, then use what's left over to handle my personal expenses and with a little luck maybe one day in the future I can invest. It wasn't bad advice; it just wasn't the right advice to be giving an ambitious young entrepreneur. The advice that financial planner was giving me would have kept me in the rat race struggling and it would have doomed me to the honey bee syndrome for life. I believe that you should pay yourself first, even if it's just 50 or 100 dollars a month. After you pay yourself- don't blow the money on foolish things- save it. Put that money in a separate savings account because this is the money you will need to invest in your first REIT, bond fund or mutual fund. Once you get an investment and you receive your first dividend- you will be excited, like I was. And that excitement will make you want more. So, this is what you should do; pay yourself, then pay your bills. There will not be any money left over for personal spending or just to hang out. The initial three years of investing will be tight and frugal.

It saddens my heart when I see people my age or younger relying on a government check for their livelihoods. Social Security Disability at the age of thirty because you were a crack head or heroin addict. What sense does that make? According to Robert Kiyosaki, businessman and author of Rich Dad, Poor Dad- there are nearly 100 million Americans that depend on the United States government for support. There's a long list of dependents such as postal workers, federal employees, state employees that are federally funded positions through grants, military retirees, federal employee retiree's- such as house representatives, senators, presidents, FBI, CIA, ATF, DEA, and ICE. Then there's Medicare, and Medicaid and most recently Obamacare! All of this depending hurt free enterprise. Plus, America doesn't have the surplus to sustain all of the payee's, and each year the number keeps growing.

Here's something to think about, with 100 million Americans and growing- is the number of people dependent on the government for their livelihood. Are people sacrificing freedom for the sake of welfare socialism? Financial freedom is an integral part of self-awareness. And that is true power! What would happen if the economy crashed again like in 2008? What would happen to those people that depend on the government check if the government shut down for 6 to 8 months? The checks from the government and its sense of security was designed to keep you poor and ignorant. You are a victim to the system that was designed to push you deeper into the rat race and the honey bee syndrome. People, it's not about what you make. It's about how much you can keep. It is about building these four elements listed below.

- Portfolio Income 1. Concentrate your investments – focus on one or even a couple small investments at a time and then build from there. REITS, Mutual funds, and ownership percentages of other people businesses.
  - Business Cashflow Income 2. Build a small business – Brand your name, promote your niche, start in your city and expand.
- Passive Income 3. Purchase Real Estate; rental units, apartment buildings, single family homes, flats, storage units. All of these create a very nice passive income.
- Charity 4. Start a non-profit or partner with one. Either way, you must give back. Just as the Lord has blessed you, you must also go out and bless others.

There are three things in life that I can guarantee that you will either be or do- without a doubt.
1. Be the race(color) you are.
2. Pay taxes.
3. And Die.

Other than those three things, life has no guarantees. So therefore, it is imperative that you take action- learn to embrace change, harness risk, and strive for good health. We will talk more about risk.

I remember when I first started working, I was fourteen years old, as page clerk- stacking books on the library shelves for $5.65 per hour- that was minimum wage back then in 1990. I was ecstatic when I got that job. I had my own money; I could buy my own things. But after the newness wore off, I realized that this wasn't no life at all. My friends were hanging out, having fun, while I was stuck stacking books onto the

library shelves. I had no freedom. It was at that moment as a
kid, that I knew that I would never find the perfect job for me.
I also knew that I wanted financial independence. The problem
that I faced was that I had no real guidance in my home (while
growing up) to teach me good business skills, or to nurture
my entrepreneurial spirit. My father was a hustler and he was
either too drunk to talk or out hustling. My mother only knew
to go to school and get a degree and then maybe you can get a
good job. My mom wanted to play it safe. I love and respect
my mom for her perseverance to give us a better life. My
mother is a retired school teacher and my father was murdered
when I was sixteen, he was thirty-nine. Neither of them never
inspired me to become wealthy. Nor did they encourage my
sense of business and independence. It's not their fault- they
were only doing what their parents had taught them.   So, I ask
you, what type of message are you sending to your children?
Are you inspiring them? What are you telling them to do with
their lives? Working a job is good. Going to college is great.
But why are they working? Is it to gain experience so that they
can run their own company? Why are they going to college?
Is it to become well educated and run their own company?
Or is it to learn how be a good robot and make someone else
companies rich? We will never be able to achieve greatness
unless we break the cycles of poor money management, lack of
education, no guidance and lack of proper financial education
for our children.

Let's talk more about risk. Risk is a necessary factor of
doing business. Everything in this life has a risk and a reward.
However, in order for you to be capable enough to deal with
risk- you must first condition your mind with positive thoughts
and actions. And you must learn to strategize and think twice

before you make a move. These things are not always easy
to do because humans are flawed by emotions that sometimes
override our best judgement and get us into bad situations.

In order to change our thought process, you must be willing
to get rid of the old friends. Those old friends are also old
habits and old routines. Those old friends are going absolutely
nowhere in life. And guess what? They want some company
to join them as they travel down their miserable road of despair
and confusion. You must align yourself with people that want
what you want. You must make new friends, travel with the
circle of people that want peace and are going places. Cut your
losses and lose the losers. My grandma used to say, "birds
of a feather, flock together." As I got older, it dawned on me
what she meant; it's quite comical now, as I reflect on how she
would chuckle, then ask me in her most southern twang voice,
"do you see giraffes hanging out with sheep? Are the peacocks
soaring with the eagles?"

I would shake my head and respond with an upbeat, "No
ma'am." And my grandma would smile at me and continue
cooking.

The lesson is, watch the company you keep and control
your risk. Once we learn that risk is something that's going
to always be present. Risk is nothing but fear of self; doubt
of your own capabilities. We must also be willing to change
with the times. We are no longer living in the industrial age.
We are living in the information age, a world that is driven by
computers, apps, and electronics. Everything is constantly
changing around us- nothing is secure, computer hackers
can assure you of that. Embrace risk as a challenge to be
conquered. Use the opportunity of failure as stepping stones
for success.

- 10 -
Poor or Disadvantaged

As I've matured throughout life, I've noticed how senti-
mental I've become. I care more now than ever before about
what happens to people, animals, and the earth. I think it's
fascinating that I'm in touch with my soul and I can express
it with tears of joy. Gone are the tears of sorrow, hurt, shame,
disappointment, guilt, pain or regret. These tears are an expres-
sion of happiness, relief, freedom, peace and self-worth. These
tears are from pain turned into pleasure. Tears of maturation,
experiences of a journey that I am still on. A journey that
taps deep into that God force that dwells deep within all of us.
These are tears of comfort because I know who the Creator is
and I also know that HE has been protecting me from the street
life, orchestrating my life for the moment that we are in now.
Defeat is temporary but giving up makes it permanent! We've
all suffered the disgrace and agonizing embarrassment from the
lashing whip of defeat. We've all lost something or someone at
some point in our lives. But it's how we handle that loss, while
enduring the pain is what defines our character.

I never would've guessed in a million years how powerful
and profound a persons' thoughts can be. It was my thoughts
and will power that pulled me out of the gutter, out of poverty,

and straight into God's grace. And it is God (also known as ALLAH, JEHOVA, ELOHIM, YAH-WEH) that has blessed my wife and I with wealth. Being poor is a state of mind. It is a conditioned way of thinking. The thinking are thoughts of insecurity, suppressed negative feelings, volatile behaviors, confused or misdirected aggression and pure rage. Angry at the system- the government. Well yes, in theory that would be the logical description of what being poor is. However, it is more intricate than that.

According to Webster's dictionary, the word poor is defined as; lacking sufficient money to live at a standard considered comfortable or normal in a society; of low or inferior standard or quality; deficient, substandard. Ironically, these definitions describe the plight and social economic challenges that the majority of the black people in the United States are confined to everyday. The black community and predominantly black neighborhoods have been the target of destruction since the days of J. Edgar Hoover, dating back to 1956, with his savage aggressive attacks to shut down black owned bookstores. And then later, turning the FBI's counter-intelligence division into the department that would spearhead investigations and target key black figures such as Malcom X, Martin Luther King Jr., Stokely Carmichael and Elijah Muhammad. Hoover's intentions were to shut down the Black Power movement and stop the rise of the next Black Messiah.

I want you to understand that every race of people on this planet know who we (Black people) are but us. Everyone in the world know that we are still asleep in a cursed slumber- allowed by God due to our wicked ways, idolatry, promiscuity, and arrogance. So, our enemy has been allowed to reign for 1,000 years. But now, God has allowed some of the original

Hebrews to awaken because Satan's permitted time is almost up. There are wicked forces in this world that will do horrendous things to keep Black people (the original Hebrew) asleep and at a disadvantage. Things such as falsification of documents, altering information and history, slavery, riots, warfare, terrorism, theft and murder. The wicked forces will also crush anyone who empathize or sympathize with the social-economic plight of Black people. The best way to contain and suppress anyone is to keep them poor and mis-informed. And the best way to do that is to keep them distracted. While they are distracted- the enemy can further execute their plan to keep you at a disadvantage. According to Webster's dictionary, the word disadvantage is defined as; 'an unfavorable circumstance or condition that reduces the chances of success or effectiveness.' Obstacles, stumbling blocks, snag, drawback- are all words you use every day when you are faced with problems that are beyond your intelligence that causes you to be distracted.

So, what are we distracted with or by? We are distracted by a combination of things and issues. Let's start with sex and sexuality. Do you find it odd that since the year 2,000 the music has gotten raunchier, and nastier, as the women are showing more butt and skin just to get attention? Mental illness, depression, porn and lust have the entire planet distracted and in complete chaos. Although I am thankful for every lesson and every blessing that the Lord, God has allowed me to experience, I can't help but wonder why so many people are homeless in the United States. These are the true disadvantaged people and very few people will ever come to their aide.

I once was disadvantaged intellectually, financially, and spiritually. It's a very dark and lonely place to be in your mind. I can relate to the agony that one must feel as they wake up every day- wishing for a better life. Its painful to wake up every day knowing that there's a better way of life, cleaner lifestyle- no drugs, positive experiences and brighter days. I also can relate to the let down and disappointment that's felt once you realize that you don't know how to escape from this nightmare. I also know how it feels to be at a disadvantage of not knowing and not having the correct information available to you. Without proper spiritual guidance, navigating through this circular world of sin can make the future seem desolate.

Yes indeed, race does play a role in keeping the disadvantaged at a disadvantage. There is a war going on it is about race. The issue of race becomes more complex because of Nazi extremist and their radical verbiage- 'make America great again propaganda' -resonating soundwaves of hate, bigotry, sexism, and racism. The reason why being disadvantaged is a complex issue now is because- the poverty from being disadvantaged has crossed all racial barriers, making this a people problem- not just a black or brown thing. However, I warn you, do not be fooled the Nazi extremist have filtered into our government agencies; the military, the United States senate, federal, state and local police. Once they are in the positions of power their goal is to execute the agenda of open boarders, one world banking by government and the total destruction of black, yellow and brown people.

Here is the five hundred-million-dollar question. What are the unfavorable conditions or circumstance that is reducing the chances of success or effectiveness among and within the minority communities? The system of America's hatred towards any one that isn't Caucasian runs deep and is embedded in the minds of those running the country. Mix a lack of education or miseducation with crack cocaine, heroin, and poverty, then what you will find is ravished Black and Latino communities. To describe what it is to be a Blackman in America is just as hypocritical as America itself, the Constitution, and the emancipation proclamation. America's hypocrisy is the root of the white supremacy mind set. The white supremacy mind set spills over into subconscious minds of blacks and other minority groups- which creates an inferiority complex or slave mentality (blacks hate blacks). The slave mentality is the reason why Black people address one another as 'nigga'. It's also the reason for all of the killings going on in Chicago as of 2017-2019. Blacks were never meant to be free. Only when we can learn to love ourselves that the genocide will stop and then other races will respect us.

- 11 -
The Power of God

Life is the most valuable element on this planet. Although some people never truly get the opportunity to appreciate all of the joys and rewards that life can bring- it's a blessing from God that we are allowed to awaken to a beautiful sunrise. As the crisp breeze gently blows through my window and the aroma of freshly brewed coffee tickles my nose- it is those moments that I am most grateful. I am also thankful for all of the painful lessons that God has allowed me to endure. Without those lessons, I am not the Roland Troutman that love God entirely.

As I reflect on how far I've come, I can't help but take notice of the fact that God gives everyone a season. Everyone has a winning season and a losing season. During the losing season it seem as though times will never get better and you feel as if you are cursed and doomed to live a life of sin and danger. But in reality, you are being fine-tuned and prepared to embrace your winning season. My mother kicked me out of the house at four-teen years old. My uncle who was addicted to crack cocaine introduced me to the drug game and taught me how to steal. At the age of six-teen my best friend was murdered. When I turned seven-teen my father was murdered.

I became immersed in the streets and committed a bank robbery that eventually led to me being imprisoned for six long years. But God always has a plan and He was there protecting me numerous times during very dangerous situations, making sure that I made it out okay. Indeed, God had a plan for me. God also has a plan for you.

My brightest moment was the birth of my daughter, Rylei. My proudest moment was the day that I married my wife, Jane. I never knew how to love until I met her. A message to all men- a strong woman by your side, one that's loyal and intelligent will turn your goodness into greatness. She will help you achieve accomplishments beyond your wildest dreams. So first find her and then make sure she's the **_Right_** one, and if she is; invest in her with your love, respect, commitment, and never let her go. Before I met my wife, I was ambitious, but I didn't know my truest potential. She also invested in me and helped me become the best that I can be. Although I have a very dark past, I never let that stop me from defining my self-worth. So, I ask you, do you know what you're worth? Do you know the value of your life? How valuable is your time? During times of hardship who can you count on? Take a moment to reflect, write your answers down on paper.

It's time to stop the rollercoaster ride. When you allow God to manifest himself entirely in your life, blessing's rain down abundantly. You also embark upon new opportunities. You start to feel better mentally, physically, emotionally and spiritually. Thank God for a sound and stable body and a pure and healthy mind. You will have victory amongst your enemies and glory beyond your wildest dreams. You will experience what it feels like to really be loved unconditionally. Along with this book, I encourage you to pick up the Bible.

If you have difficulty understanding because of the language and terminology- I suggest the New International Version- it's written in plain English and is easy to understand. Begin your reading in Genesis, take notes, ask questions, but most of all pray. Pray to God that he gives you wisdom to understand and receive His holy word into your spirit. As you being to grow financially- you will need spiritual food to keep you humble and grounded. Stay away from reckless people with self-destructive, hateful attitudes. I'd like to share with you some scriptures that has been very effective. These scriptures help build character, self-esteem as well as spiritual wisdom. 'A simple man believes in anything but a prudent man gives thought prior to his actions. A wise man fears the Lord and shun the spirits of evil. But a fool is hot headed and reckless.' Proverbs Chapter 14, verses 15 and 16.

It is better to give thought to all of your possibilities before jumping to conclusions. Weigh your options, decide what is best for you and your family because in the end that is all that will matter. Remain disciplined, with self-control. Don't lose your cool in volatile situations, instead practice strategy over strength.

As proof that you will be rewarded for doing the Lord's will- read Psalms 37 scriptures 3, 4, and 5; "Trust in the Lord and do good; dwell in the land and enjoy safe pasture. Delight yourself in the Lord and He will give you the desires of your heart. Commit your ways to the Lord; Trust in Him and He will make your righteousness shine like the dawn and your cause like the noon day sun."

In other words, we all have fallen short to the glory of God because we are of the flesh. Because we are of the flesh- we were born into a world of sin. Although we were born into sin and we quite often live immoral our destiny is with God. It is because of our flesh and sin of this world that we are, by nature, considered evil; weak with no self-control. All of us on this planet, to some degree are immoral and sin daily- even the Pope. The Pope is an honorable man- but still he is only a man and he has sinned. Only Jesus was perfect, without sin and lived a morally righteous life. Jesus is our only perfect example. Most of us are aware of the battle between good and evil that has existed since the beginning of time. However, when dealing in the realm of business and politics, the lines of morality are often blurred for the sake of making money. We must never sell our soul. We are to remain morally strong and spiritually conscious; aware and capable of the power of God. Submit your entire self to serving God and you will find success in your marriages, your family life will be more fulfilling, you will find success in your job, career and in the business world of entrepreneurs. Be careful not to make immorality your reality.

Zechariah Chapter 8 verses 16 and 17 explains; These are the things you should do; 'speak the truth to each other, and render true and sound judgement in your courts. Do not plot evil against your neighbor and do not swear falsely, I hate all of this', declares the Lord.

God has no gray area- either you are all the way in or you are all the way out! He's too righteous and too pure to allow immorality to even be near His presence. I must also warn you about the power of words. Words give life to our actions. It is our actions caused by our flawed character, which actually brings about negativity, anger, disruptive behavior, swearing and immoral sex. All of these things are considered sins. As the scripture explains, "be very careful how you live- not as the unwise, making the most of every opportunity because their days are evil. Therefore, do not be foolish but understand what the Lord's will is."- Ephesians chapter 5 verses 15,16, and 17.

Understanding! It is that one word – 'understanding'- that is the key to unlocking all of God's blessings that is intended for you. But you must understand God in order to obey God. We must learn to overlook some things and some people. The best way to do that is to start developing patience. Well, you may ask, 'how do we develop patience?' Patience is gained through growth in your walk with God, love and wisdom. And wisdom is only gained through prayer and experience. Wisdom is one of God's most beloved angels.

"A man's wisdom gives him patience; it is to his glory to overlook an offense." – Proverbs chapter 19 verses 11.

There is a huge void in the world. That void is love. We all suffer from too much hate and pain. As we exercise our freedoms, I've realized that there is not enough love because of the freedom to be over indulgent in the expressions of self. But the fact remains, that freedom has a price. Humans by nature desire freedom. Freedom throughout history has never been accomplished by being silent. Therefore, by the character of choice embedded within all of us, we fight for our very lives- to live the way we choose. Civil order is never civil- it is practically violent! With violence and force we understand that there is always going to be a dominant group. The dominant group- in most cases- usually dictates the laws and order.

Intriguing enough, I found it interesting that in the United States of America there are multiple layers and sub fractioned dominant groups in almost everything that goes on in this country, except for politics. So, I ask you, can a judge preside over a case in a fair manner without allowing their

personal beliefs interfere with their moral character? Do we-
as followers of the Lord God Jehovah- always make the best
choices based upon what is morally and spiritually right? One
might argue that spiritual and moral righteousness is common
sense. Some may even agree with that. However, from my
experiences here on earth, I've found that common sense cannot
be taken for granted because everyone doesn't have common
sense- the ability to make rational, positive, safe choices effec-
tively and immediately. I've also realized that everyone will
not learn at the same pace and simultaneously understanding
that it is our concepts and views that dictate what we ultimately
consider to be moral. What we consider to be moral is based
on a simpler level of how we perceive situations and things in
life. Much of that perception is based on what we believe to be
common sense- something that everyone should already know,
sort of like an unwritten rule of understanding.

I've also discovered is that liberals and conservatives or
democrats and republicans are not true to anything but their
own bank accounts and self-interest. In fact, the republican
and democrat politicians are on the same side- most are a part
of a bigger scheme and network that control all of the current
world leaders, except China's and North Korea's leaders. By
no means am I angry- I merely understand the level of corrup-
tion that will never be tamed and the working-class citizen will
continue to be trapped in a matrix, a world of illusions and
distractions, as the politicians play us like a fiddle. In all reality
nothing is as it appears to be. There is never a conflict. The
conflicts are created by the people in power to keep the unin-
formed and poor divided. Do what is morally right. There is
only one righteousness. One morality. And that's the power of
God.

Words have a different meaning depending on who you are talking to. Since we know that this is Satan's world, we must protect ourselves. We must put on the full armor of God and breast plate of righteousness and arm ourselves with the sword of God (our Bible).

We must never sell our souls for the sake of making money. It's okay to be wealthy as long as you are walking in the path of righteousness and your intentions and actions are positive. Respect the value of money but never fall in love with it.

"For we brought nothing in this world, and we can take nothing out of it. But if we have food and clothing, we will be content, with that. People who want to get rich fall into temptation and a trap and into many foolish and harmful desires that plunge men into ruin and destruction. For the love of money is the root of all kinds of evil. Some people, eager for money have wandered from the faith and pierced themselves with many griefs". (1st Timothy chapter 6 verses 7 through 10).

I write my books because I want to make a positive difference in people's lives. I write my books because the Lord has allowed me to prosper and I want to help others become their greatest being. My books are intended for the poor, the struggling, the hopeless, the helpless, the dreamer and the lonely. I write my books as a witness that Christ is alive and that God can change anyone if He changed me. Use me as your example and proof that you can find success at the end of the road, if you just keep traveling. I've also witnessed God's mercy and that's how I learned to respect life. And once you learn how to respect life, then you will be capable of respecting all people. In closing, when someone attempt to destroy your dreams, tell you that you can't do it- or predicts your doom or belittle you- just remember- they are telling you their story, not yours.

Time is the essence of all things. Everything begins and ends with time. It does not think or talk and it dictates without a will or conscience. Time waits for no one!

—Roland E. Troutman Jr.